Cliques, Crushes, & True Friends

Developing Healthy Relationships

ABDO
Publishing Company

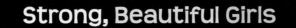

Strong, Beautiful Girls

Cliques, Crushes, & True Friends

Developing Healthy Relationships

by Ashley Rae Harris

Content Consultant
Vicki F. Panaccione, PhD
Licensed Child Psychologist
Founder, Better Parenting Institute

Credits

Published by ABDO Publishing Company, 8000 West 78th Street, Edina, Minnesota 55439. Copyright © 2009 by Abdo Consulting Group, Inc. International copyrights reserved in all countries. No part of this book may be reproduced in any form without written permission from the publisher. The Essential Library™ is a trademark and logo of ABDO Publishing Company.

Printed in the United States.

Special thanks to Dr. Vicki Panaccione for her expertise and guidance in shaping this series.

Editor: Erika Wittekind
Copy Editor: Patricia Stockland
Interior Design and Production: Becky Daum, Nicole Brecke
Cover Design: Becky Daum

Library of Congress Cataloging-in-Publication Data
Harris, Ashley Rae.
  Cliques, crushes & true friends : developing healthy relationships / by Ashley Rae Harris.
    p. cm. — (Essential health : strong, beautiful girls)
  Includes index.
  ISBN 978-1-60453-099-5
  1. Interpersonal relations. 2. Teenage girls—Psychology. I. Title. II. Title: Cliques, crushes, and friends.

BF724.3.I58H37 2008
155.5'33—dc22
                                    2008012103

Contents

Meet Dr. Vicki

Throughout the series Strong, Beautiful Girls, you'll hear the reassuring, knowledgeable voice of Dr. Vicki Panaccione, a licensed psychologist with more than 25 years of experience working with teens, children, and families. Dr. Vicki offers her expert advice to girls who find themselves in the difficult situations described in each chapter.

Better known as the Parenting Professor™, Dr. Vicki is founder of the Better Parenting Institute™ and author of *Discover Your Child* and *What Your Kids Would Tell You . . . If Only You'd Ask!* You might have seen her name quoted in publications such as the *New York Times*, *Family Circle*, and *Parents* magazine.

While her credentials run deep, perhaps what qualifies her most to advise girls on everything from body image to friendship to schoolwork is that she's been there, so she can relate. "I started out in junior high as the chubby new kid with glasses and freckles, who the popular kids loved to tease or even worse . . . ignore," says the doc. "They should see me now!"

Today, Dr. Vicki maintains a private practice in Melbourne, Florida, and writes articles for a variety of periodicals and Web sites. She has been interviewed or quoted in major publications including *Parenting* magazine, *Reader's Digest*, *First for Women*, and *Woman's World*, networks such as Fox, ABC, NBC, and CBS, and several popular Web sites. Dr. Vicki joined esteemed colleagues Tony Robbins, Dr. Wayne Dyer, and Bill Bartmann as coauthor of *The Power of Team*, the latest in the best-selling series Wake Up and Live the Life You Love. She is an adviser for the Web site parentalwisdom.com and also for MTV/Nickelodeon's parentsconnect.com. She is a clinical consultant for Red Line Editorial, Inc. Not to mention, she's the proud mother of Alex, her 21-year-old son who is pursuing his PhD to become a medical researcher.

   With all that she has going for her now, it might be hard to imagine that Dr. Vicki was ever an awkward teen struggling to find her way. But consider this—she's living proof that no matter how bleak things might look now, they do get better. The following stories and Dr. Vicki's guidance will help you discover your own path to happiness and success, becoming the Strong, Beautiful Girl you are meant to be.

Take It from Me

Who are the most important people in your life? If you didn't say your family, then you probably said your friends. Most adolescent girls put friendship at the top of their list of priorities. This should come as no surprise—you need someone who knows all about you, but who will never ground you because of it. Good friends are awesome. They'll listen to you when you need to talk and laugh with you when you need to have fun. Good friends also will watch your back when other kids give you a hard time.

Good friends are so important that it can be devastating if you find yourself without them. Unfortunately, this time in your life brings many changes, and that includes changing friendships. You may be super close with a girl one year and not even talk to her the next. You may find yourself torn when your friends want to do something you know is wrong. Your group might drop you out of the blue. You may struggle to define a relationship with a close guy friend when everyone expects you to hang out only with other girls. And you are almost guaranteed to find yourself in different roles depending on the situation. You could be the leader, the follower, the nice one, and the bully—all in the same week!

Part of the reason why there is so much excitement and disappointment in your social life is because you are changing so much, and so is everyone else around you. You are starting to make independent choices about the kind of person you want to be. That means you also are making decisions about the people with whom you hang out. It isn't as simple as spending your time with the drama club versus the soccer team. This is your life we're talking about here!

Even though you probably will get your feelings hurt by a friend or a peer at least a few times during adolescence, there is a lot of fun to be had, too. More importantly, you will learn about yourself in the process. I hope this book will help you define what kind of a friend you want to be and give you ideas for smart ways to handle the different situations that may come up.

Don't bother thanking me—that's what friends are for!

XOXO,
Ashley

1

The Follower

Twenty years ago, it seemed like the after-school specials on television were always talking about peer pressure. Some kid with a joint would be trying to get another kid to smoke it. The girl would be scared at first, but she'd do it anyway, and within a week she'd become a full-blown drug addict. At the time, it seemed to me that whoever was writing the story lines for these shows didn't have a clue what kids were really about. For one thing, most peer pressure situations aren't so obvious. Rather than one kid forcing another kid to do something illegal, it's more likely that a girl would be torn between doing what she knows is right and trying something just to fit in.

For another thing, most preteens and teens are somewhat insecure and unsure of themselves during adolescence. They tend to respect those who are leaders and who speak up for what they believe in more than those who simply follow the crowd.

Peer pressure for girls is often different and in many ways crueler than it is for boys. Whereas a group of boys may pressure another boy to do something gross or dangerous for entertainment, groups of girls are likely to gang up on one girl in more subtle and long-lasting ways. Other girls might talk about her behind her back, ignore her at school, not invite her to a party everyone else is invited to, or make her feel like an untouchable.

Peer pressure for girls is often different and in many ways crueler than it is for boys.

The worst part is that she won't find relief until another girl takes her place.

Obviously, no one wants to be in that position. Girls are willing to say and do terrible things to other girls to avoid being picked on themselves. Whether you're the leader, the follower, or somewhere in between, chances are you'll find yourself participating in this drama at some point during adolescence.

So, how can you stay cool with your friends without hurting someone else? Amanda had to answer the same question. Read on to find out how she handled it.

Amanda's Story

Amanda was a nice girl. She had many friends and was in three different clubs at school. She was definitely part of the popular group, which consisted of three other girls: Liz, Kiki, and Amanda's closest friend, Brit. Amanda and Brit grew up on the same block and had been friends since they were little kids. Brit didn't always have the best clothes or the right haircut, and Amanda knew that Brit was part of the group mostly because of their friendship.

Liz was definitely the leader of the foursome. She looked older than the other girls, with bigger breasts and more expensive clothes. Her dad made a lot of money, and Liz had the girls over all the time to sun-bathe and swim in her pool.

Kiki was Liz's closest friend. She was always around, and she was pretty much up for whatever Liz wanted to do. Amanda thought of her as Liz's sidekick.

Toward the end of the seventh grade, Liz started inviting Amanda over to swim without Kiki and Brit. She said she was annoyed with Kiki for always follow-ing her around. Amanda felt guilty for leaving the other girls out, but she had fun going over to Liz's house by herself. Liz seemed less bossy and paid more attention to her when it was just the two of them. Amanda could tell it bugged Brit when she wasn't invited along, but neither of them said anything about it. They still hung out and ate lunch together at school. Meanwhile, Kiki would call and try to invite herself over, which annoyed Liz even more.

Talk About It

- Do you have friends who act differently one-on-one than they act in a group? How so?

- In your group, are you the leader, the follower, or somewhere in between?

- Do you have a best friend? What made you decide she was your best friend?

One afternoon Brit called Amanda and asked her if she wanted to go to the mall to shop for summer sandals. Liz had already invited Amanda to come over and hang out by the pool, but Amanda didn't want to tell Brit that.

"I'd love to, but I think my mom is making me help around the house," Amanda said instead.

"Too bad," Brit said. "I hope we can hang out sometime soon. I've been missing you."

Amanda felt guilty about the lie, but she soon forgot about it. Later, at the pool, Liz started talking about the other girls. They were having a particularly fun time laughing and talking when Liz asked Amanda, "Doesn't it ever bug you that Brit wants to be just like you? She acts like Kiki."

Amanda didn't know what to say. She and Brit had been friends for what seemed like forever. But she had to admit, she sometimes just wanted to do her own thing.

Amanda didn't know what to say. She and Brit had been friends for what seemed like forever. They didn't even knock when they went over to each other's houses. But she had to admit, she sometimes just wanted to do her own thing. She hated it when Brit seemed bummed about Amanda going over to Liz's by herself.

"I don't know. I guess sometimes I just want to do my thing without having to worry about her," Amanda said.

"See! That's exactly what I mean! Some girls are hot, and other girls are just nothings. Obviously, we're in the hot category!"

It was supposed to be funny, and Amanda laughed along. She was flattered that Liz thought of her as hot, but she felt guilty talking about Brit and Kiki behind their backs. She knew Brit would never say anything bad about her.

Talk About It

- Have you ever said something behind a friend's back that you knew would hurt her to hear? How did you feel?

- Have you ever had a friend pressure you to say something mean about someone else?

"You know what we should do? We should have a party and not invite them, just to see what they'll do," Liz said next.

Now Amanda felt even guiltier. It was one thing to go over to Liz's house without her, but it was another to have a party and not invite Brit. She knew Kiki would be totally hurt too.

"That would be so mean!" Amanda said, laughing nervously.

"Well, at least they'd finally get the hint," Liz said, shrugging.

Amanda tried to change the subject, but Liz kept on, making an invitation list that included a bunch of cute boys and some eighth grade girls. It would be a pool party, so they could wear their cutest bikinis in front of the boys they liked. Amanda had to admit she was excited about it, even though she felt bad about leaving Brit out.

As the date for the party neared, Amanda began to avoid Brit. She didn't answer Brit's calls and was quiet during lunch so she wouldn't have to talk about it. A few times Brit tried to bring it up, and Amanda just said, "I don't know. It's not my party." But she knew that was only a half-truth.

Talk About It

- Have you ever avoided a friend? Why did you do it, and how did it make you feel?

- Has a friend ever excluded you from a social event? How did you handle the situation?

- Is a half-truth really the truth or a lie? Why?

Finally the day of the party had come. Amanda and Liz hung out waiting for the guests and picking out sandals that matched their bathing suits. Liz let Amanda borrow her favorite white shorts, which she said made Amanda look sexy. Amanda was having such a good time that she almost forgot about Brit and Kiki.

But when the eighth grade girls showed up, Liz started to ignore Amanda. Amanda felt like a total dork just standing there while Liz talked to everyone but her. She didn't know how to join the conversation because she didn't know anyone.

After a while, she started to wish Brit were there. She even missed Kiki.

After the party was over, Liz was back to normal, talking to Amanda and gushing about how much fun she'd had. She asked Amanda to sleep over, but Amanda didn't want to anymore.

When Amanda got home, she called Brit right away.

"Hey, do you want to hang out?" she asked Brit.

"I don't know if I really feel like it," Brit said. Amanda could hear the hurt in her voice and suddenly felt terrible about leaving her out.

"The party wasn't that fun," Amanda told her.

"Why am I not surprised?" Now Brit sounded angry.

"I'm sorry that we didn't invite you. I missed you today," Amanda told her.

"I would never have done that to you, you know," said Brit.

"Do you still want to be friends?" Amanda asked quietly.

"I guess you can come over if you want. Kiki's here," Brit said.

Amanda felt so relieved to hang out with Brit and Kiki and grateful that they were willing to forgive her. She vowed never to exclude either of them again. She realized being popular wasn't worth losing her best friend.

Talk About It

- Do you think Brit forgave Amanda too easily? How would you have handled the situation if you were Brit?

- How do you think Liz will treat Amanda now that she is friends with Brit and Kiki again?

- Have you ever done something that hurt a good friendship? Were you able to get it back? What did you do?

Amanda let peer pressure get the better of her, but she was lucky to get her friend back when she realized her mistake. Adolescent girls often define themselves by who their friends are. Amanda was flattered that someone who seemed cooler and more popular had chosen her as a best friend. Many times it is not just pressure from another person or group that affects a girl's decisions during adolescence. It also is an internal desire to try something different or to be someone else. Like many girls, Amanda ended up wanting to go back to what was comfortable and safe after the thrill of hanging out with Liz had worn off.

It is perfectly normal and healthy for girls to experiment with different social groups, but they shouldn't feel like they have to hurt anyone else in the process. The most well-adjusted girls are able to be friends with lots of different kids without having to compromise their sense of right and wrong or hurt anyone in the process.

Get Healthy

1. In most peer pressure situations, you are not the only one who is uncomfortable. Practice speaking up and saying what you really think. You may be surprised that other people follow your lead.

2. To make the most out of your social life, try hanging out with different types of people. You'll learn about new things, and you won't feel like you need one particular group to be cool.

3. Ask yourself how you would handle peer pressure so that you have a plan ready. What would you do if someone offered you alcohol or drugs? What would you do if someone asked you to turn your back on a friend?

4. It can be hard to break into a new group, so if someone new tries to join your group, give her a chance.

The Last Word from Ashley

A lot of the peer pressures that adolescent girls experience have to do with belonging to a social group. Girls compete for the role of most popular, or simply try to make sure they aren't labeled a dork. It's fine to experiment with different social groups to figure out where you belong, but that doesn't mean you have to choose just one friend or group. If someone is mean to one girl, think of how you'd feel in her place. And if your friends ask you to do something that feels wrong, or they won't respect your decision to say no, then maybe they're not really your friends after all.

2

The Best Boy Friend

Considering how cruel girls can be to one another, wouldn't it be easier to just be friends with boys? Boys don't care about gossip. They just want to hang out and have fun, right? Any girl who has close guy friends in middle school knows that it's not quite that simple. While friendships with boys may be easier in some ways, they also can be way more complicated. One of you might start to develop romantic feelings for the other. Some kids might accuse you of dating. Sometimes, other kids might even accuse one of you of being gay. If you can get past all the drama, you might find you really like hanging out with boys sometimes. These friendships might even be among the most important in your life.

Dani enjoyed hanging out with her best friend, Christian, but the relationship got more complicated when kids at school started talking about them. Dani found herself in the tricky situation of showing Christian he could trust her amidst the rumors.

Dani's Story

Dani was a laid-back girl who loved '80s pop music. She had a huge collection of just about every '80s dance song that had ever been written. Her best friend, Christian, would come over almost every day, and they would listen to them in her room. Dani and Christian had been friends since they were little. Neither of them were social butterflies, but Dani knew a few girls she liked to hang out with sometimes. Christian, on the other hand, had no real friends besides Dani.

Dani liked hanging out with Christian because she felt like she could totally be herself around him.

Dani liked hanging out with Christian more than anyone else because she felt like she could totally be herself around him. The two spent so much time together that people at school saw them as a unit. Usually it wasn't that big a deal, but sometimes their relationship seemed to bug other kids.

"Are you guys, like, doing it or something?" asked Jenny one day at school.

"No, they're not doing it," said a kid named Travis. "Christian just hangs out with Dani because he wants to be a girl. He's gay. Are you gay too, Dani?" Several people laughed. Dani felt her face turn bright red. She wanted to hide.

Dani felt her face turn bright red.

Talk About It

- Do you have any friends who are boys? What do you enjoy about your friendship with them? Is there anything you don't like?

- Have other kids ever assumed you were dating or fooling around with a boy just because you were hanging out with him?

- Have other kids ever asked you personal questions about your sexuality? How did it make you feel?

What Travis said bothered Dani. She knew he was a major jerk, and she hated it when people said mean things about Christian, but she thought part of what he said might be true. Dani had considered the fact that Christian might hang out with her because he was seriously uncomfortable around other guys, and that maybe he was uncomfortable because he was a

little bit on the girly side. He didn't dress like a girl or anything—he just didn't act all tough or macho, make fart jokes, or play violent video games.

Dani couldn't care less if Christian wore a baseball cap or a pink shirt—she just really enjoyed his company and his sense of humor. But, she was worried about how the rumors might affect Christian, and she didn't want her classmates thinking she was gay. She worried that if everyone thought that, then no boys would want to date her for the rest of middle school or high school.

Talk About It

- Have you ever worried that people might judge you because of who your friends are? How did you handle it?

- What do you think Dani should do next? Should she talk to Christian about what's going on?

- Do you have any gay friends? How would you feel if you found out one of your friends was gay?

One day, Christian came over to watch a reality show about fashion designers.

"This is totally my favorite show!" he said enthusiastically as they nestled into the couch to watch.

"Christian, do you ever think you might be gay?" Dani said, laughing. She meant it as a joke, but she regretted saying it when she saw that Christian wasn't laughing along.

"I'm just kidding," she said quickly, and changed the subject. Christian didn't say anything about it, but during the rest of the show, there was an awkward vibe in the room. Dani felt bad that she made Christian uncomfortable. Maybe he really was gay. She wanted him to know that she didn't care one way or the other, but she had no idea how to bring it up. She was afraid that if she said anything, Christian would just get quiet again.

For some time, Dani forgot about the whole thing. One day the two of them were listening to music in her room and talking about people from school. Dani had just finished telling Christian all about the guy she liked who completely ignored her.

"I don't know why you even like that jerk. You are way cooler than he is, and you wear better jeans," Christian said with a bit of a smirk.

"Do you like anyone?" Dani asked tentatively.

"Not really. I don't know."

"You know," Dani said carefully, "if you liked anyone, anyone at all, you could tell me. I wouldn't care who, as long as they had decent taste in music."

"Thanks, Dani," Christian said. Even though she hadn't asked him directly whether he wanted to date boys, she felt good that she had told Christian that he could trust her. She was sure that if he wanted to talk about anything, he would come to her when he was ready.

Talk About It

- **How do you think Dani handled the situation? Would you trust her with a secret if you were her friend?**

- **Which of your friends do you trust the most? Who do you trust the least? Why?**

- **How are gay kids treated in your school?**

Ask Dr. Vicki

Talking about sexuality is often difficult and uncomfortable, especially when you and your friends first start to think about sexual feelings and dating. Dani might have been a little bit insensitive when she laughed about the possibility of Christian being gay. But later, she found a way to let him know that she cared about him whether or not he was gay, without putting him on the spot.

If you can accept your friends for who they are, they may be your friends for life. Sometimes, however, you might discover things about your friends that make you uncomfortable or are difficult to accept. Just as a lot of girls think they can only be friends with other girls, lots of kids grow up believing that being gay is wrong, and that they shouldn't be friends with gay kids. But just because someone is a boy or is gay doesn't mean that he can't be a great friend. It is best to judge your friends by how they treat you and whether or not you enjoy being around them.

Get Healthy

1. Try talking to boys in your classes or after-school activities who you think might be fun or cool, even if you're not interested in dating them. It can be nice to take a break from girl talk every once in a while.

2. Write down the top ten qualities that you look for in a friend. Then ask yourself if someone had all ten qualities, would it matter to you whether that person was a boy, a girl, straight, or gay? Get your priorities straight and then see who your friends turn out to be.

3. If you notice kids getting teased about their sexuality at school, try to imagine how uncomfortable that kind of harassment would make you feel. Consider sticking up for the person being teased, or at least refuse to participate yourself.

4. Think of two different ways you could show your friends that they can trust you, and then try one out. How did it affect your friendship?

The Last Word from Ashley

One of the most exciting things about getting older and building your social life is that you get to be friends with all kinds of different people. Learning to get to know people for who they really are on the inside, rather than judging them for superficial qualities, such as what they wear, can be very rewarding. Over time, you are likely to notice that many of your friends are cool in their own way, and that's why you like them. By the way, they probably like you for the same reason.

3

The Gossip Girl

rust is a key part of friendship. But what happens when a friend betrays that bond? Unfortunately, middle school can bring out the catty side of girls. It's a terrible feeling when a friend blabs a secret that you trusted her to keep private. Sometimes the betrayal is bad enough to tear the friendship apart, especially if the whole school finds out about it. It's no wonder some girls choose to keep their most personal thoughts to themselves. But, it is best to have at least one or two friends who are there for you when something is really bothering you. So, when is it safe to share a secret with a friend? What do you do if someone betrays your trust?

Read on to find out how Courtney answered these questions. She found out that to trust other girls, you have to show them they can trust you, too.

Courtney's Story

Courtney was the queen of the gossip circle at her school. Somehow, she always seemed to know which girls wanted to date which boys, who had failed a history exam, or who skipped gym class because she had her period. Because she ran the show when it came to juicy tidbits, other girls went to her when they'd heard something worth talking about.

Courtney didn't really intend to hurt anyone's feelings by spreading rumors. She just really liked being surrounded by people and entertaining them. She figured that even if someone was embarrassed for a few days, everyone would forget about it once there was something new to talk about. She'd grown up with a chatty mom and didn't see the harm in gossip—to her it was all in fun.

Courtney was the queen of the gossip circle at her school. Somehow, she always seemed to know which girls wanted to date which boys, who had failed a history exam, or who skipped gym class.

Talk About It

- Are you a gossip? Do you have friends who gossip?

- Do you think gossip is fun and harmless, or are there times when it should be taken more seriously?

- What are some of the harmful consequences of gossip? Can you think of anything good about it?

Since Courtney was usually the one to spread the latest news, it came as a surprise to her when she arrived at school to find all of her classmates buzzing around and whispering about something that she'd heard nothing about. She couldn't wait to find out what it was.

Courtney hunted down her best friend, Susan, and pulled her aside.

"What is everyone talking about this morning? It's like the cafeteria exploded or something!" Courtney laughed.

Susan looked uncomfortable. "I have no idea," she replied, shrugging. "Sorry, I have to get to class early today to study. See ya." With that, she disappeared down the hallway.

That was weird, thought Courtney. Now she was more anxious than ever to find out what was going on. She'd have to find someone else to give her a clue.

Then she spotted Corinne. Corinne was probably the only girl who could beat out Courtney with a hot new rumor.

"Hey, Corinne! Come here!" Courtney called from across the hall. The two of them were generally more competitors than friends, but occasionally they'd chat if there was something particularly juicy to discuss. Courtney figured now was one of those times. Corinne strutted over with three girls from her crowd right behind her.

"What is going on here today? Everyone is acting crazy!" Courtney said.

"Haven't you heard?"

"Heard what?!" Courtney asked, excited to get the scoop.

"Somebody's dad dated one of the math teachers last semester," Corinne said with a smug grin on her face. "Isn't that so gross?"

"And isn't that, like, illegal or something?" one of the other girls added, giggling.

Courtney suddenly felt sick to her stomach. It was her dad they were talking about. And from the way they were looking at her, she could tell everyone else knew it, too.

"I bet that's why you got an A in that class, huh?" Corinne said, and then she and her friends burst into laughter and walked away. All Courtney could do was stand there, stunned.

Talk About It

- How do you think Courtney feels? What do you think she'll do?

- Have you ever been the target of gossip? How did you feel? What did you do?

- Have you ever started gossip or spread rumors about someone? Why?

Courtney's parents divorced two years ago, and it had been devastating to her. She couldn't stand to see either one of them date new people. When her dad came home from a parent-teacher conference last fall with plans to meet Miss Stevenson that night for dinner, she couldn't imagine anything worse. Luckily, the two didn't really hit it off, and it fizzled after a few weeks. But, it ruined math class for Courtney. For the rest of the semester, she couldn't look Miss Stevenson in the eye. And she still hadn't forgiven her dad for putting her through that.

Still, Courtney didn't understand how everyone found out about it. The only person she had told was Susan, and she thought she could trust her to keep her mouth shut about something that personal.

So much for being best friends, Courtney thought angrily.

For the rest of the morning, Courtney could feel everyone's eyes on her. She assumed every whisper and snicker was about her, and she felt awful. Thinking that her best friend had caused all this humiliation made her feel even worse. At lunchtime, she found Susan at their usual table.

Had she been causing other people this much pain all along without realizing it?

"How could you do this to me?" she demanded, almost in tears. "I told you that in private, and you had no right to go blabbing it all over school!"

"I didn't!" exclaimed Susan. "I mean, I didn't mean to. Some kids were talking about how hot Miss Stevenson is and whether she had a boyfriend, and it just sort of slipped out. Anyway, I didn't think you'd mind so much. You have so much fun spreading other people's secrets."

When she thought about it like that, Courtney felt ashamed. Had she been causing other people this much pain all along without realizing it? It didn't seem worth it.

"Anyway, I'm really sorry," Susan said. "I'd take it back if I could."

After a few days, the talk died down, and Courtney felt more like her normal self. The other kids in her class started to talk to her again. Still, every time she thought about it, she felt sick to her stomach again.

Talk About It

- What would you have said to Courtney if you were in Susan's position?

- Is what Susan did understandable, considering Courtney's history? Should Courtney forgive Susan?

- Do you think this might change how much Courtney gossips in the future?

A few weeks after the incident, Courtney was working with a partner on a science experiment. They were chatting about the upcoming football game when Jill asked suddenly, "Hey, did you hear that Dave broke up with Beth? I heard it was because she wouldn't go upstairs with him at Kyle's party."

Courtney didn't know what to say. In the old days, she would have made a joke about how uptight Beth was. But after being the victim of some nasty gossip, it just wasn't as much fun to rag on other girls.

"I always thought she was nice," Courtney mumbled.

"I guess so," Jill shrugged, before changing the subject back to their assignment. After she refused to talk about Beth's love life, Courtney felt better, even if the conversation wasn't as exciting.

Courtney gained popularity by being in the know. She made herself look cooler by putting down other students. That only works as long as other people listen. Courtney ended up getting a taste of her own medicine. Luckily, it made her realize just how harmful her words could be. She was able to learn from the experience and stop contributing to the rumor mill once and for all.

Middle school can be a difficult time to make friends and be liked. Many girls feel desperate to be popular and are willing to do whatever it takes to get there. Unfortunately, too many girls believe that they have to cut other girls down to be popular. Eventually, they usually find that while they might know a lot of people, they don't have very many true friends.

Get Healthy

1. The next time someone says something cruel about a girl you know, try saying something nice instead. A lot of times, other girls are just looking for a conversation starter. When they realize that you aren't interested in gossiping, they will find something else to talk about.

2. Before you spread a rumor about another girl, ask yourself how you would feel if you were in her position. Would it be funny to you? If the answer is no, then stop yourself from saying it. Even laughing at a rumor is just as hurtful as spreading one. It's not always easy, but other girls will respect you more if you are consistently kind.

3. Instead of trying to make others laugh at the expense of another girl, challenge yourself to be truly funny. Learn how to tell a funny story about yourself. People will respond to you if you can laugh at yourself.

The Last Word from Ashley

It's easy to get sucked into the gossip in middle school. It takes strong willpower to rise above it. Girls who can avoid participating in the rumor cycle, focusing on the positive traits of others instead, tend to have a happier attitude overall. They devote more time and energy to having fun and enjoying life, and other kids are drawn to them. Ultimately, other people will treat you the way that they see you treat others. Remember, what goes around comes around. Watch what you say, or it may come back to bite you in the butt.

4

The Cling-on

No one likes to be left out, especially during adolescence when not being invited to something could mean it's time to look for a new group of friends. Some girls are so afraid of being left out that they cling to the friends they've got. You can't really blame them for wanting to hold on tight so they don't get lost at the middle school dance, but sometimes clinginess can drive people away. Girls who are too clingy strike others as insecure. Some kids might wonder why they can't just do their own thing.

Why are some girls so clingy? A girl might feel intimidated by more confident girls and decide to just go along, hoping they'll like her. She might fear getting dropped with the dorks when she would rather hang out with the popular girls. Maybe she has a history of getting ditched, either by other friends or by a parent or relative at home. Whatever the reason, it's a good idea for all girls to learn how to get along with others while still keeping their individuality.

Girls who are too clingy strike others as insecure. Some kids might wonder why they can't just do their own thing.

Vidya benefited from being friends with one of the most popular girls in school—that is, until her friend turned on her for tagging along too much. Find out how Vidya dealt with being dropped.

Vidya's Story

Just about everyone thought of Vidya as friendly and likeable. She got along well with her classmates and teachers and laughed and smiled a lot, even if she was a bit on the quiet side. She was rarely the first one to say anything negative about any of the other girls, although she hardly disagreed with any of the gossip she overheard. The middle child in a family of five kids, Vidya was used to listening and sharing, so it didn't bother her in the least to go with the flow. In fact, she usually preferred sitting on the sidelines to playing the game.

Vidya's social life was pretty basic. She wasn't the coolest girl in school, but she definitely wasn't the dorkiest. It didn't hurt that her best friend was Tiffany Baker. Tiffany was the prettiest girl in the entire sixth grade class. She had beautiful long hair and awesome jeans. Pretty much all the boys wanted to go out with her, but she spent her free time with Vidya instead.

Vidya couldn't figure out why Tiffany had chosen her as her best friend when she could be friends with anyone she wanted. But she definitely didn't want to give up her spot. Being friends with Tiffany meant she was invited to all the parties, and sometimes she was asked out by boys who were friends with the guys who liked Tiffany. The only problem with the situation was that Tiffany could be kind of mean and bossy at times. It seemed like they always had to do what Tiffany wanted. For example, Vidya was really excited when they made plans to see a new thriller one weekend, but Tiffany changed her mind at the last minute. They ended up watching the latest chick flick instead.

Talk About It

- Do you know girls like Tiffany or Vidya? Who would you say you are more like and why?

- Why do you think Tiffany is so popular? Is it because of her appearance, or could there be other reasons?

- How do you think Vidya feels about doing what Tiffany wants all the time?

Sometimes when Tiffany got in a certain mood, she would ignore Vidya and start hanging out with another friend, Jenna, instead. Jenna and Vidya would become enemies. If one of them was hanging out with Tiffany, it meant the other one wasn't. Secretly, however, Vidya kind of liked Jenna and wished they could be friends too.

Talk About It

- Why can't Vidya and Jenna be friends?
- Can you think of anyone that you dislike publicly but like privately? Why do you feel that way about them?
- Have you ever been jealous when your friend hangs out with someone else?

During one of these spells, Vidya had to partner up with another girl, Stacy, for the sixth-grade relay race. She hated watching Tiffany and Jenna laughing while she was bored and miserable on the other side of the field. It didn't even help that Stacy was a nice, fun girl who Vidya usually enjoyed.

When the gym teacher called everyone together, he began instructing the teams where to position themselves.

"Tiffany and Vidya, you start behind the goalie net," he instructed. Vidya figured he must have

assumed they'd be together since they usually were. For a second she was happy at the thought that she and Tiffany would be partners again. She knew if they hung out for the relay that they'd be friends again, and Tiffany would forget all about Jenna for a while.

"But I want to be with Jenna! She's my BFF!" Tiffany protested. She looked right at Vidya while she said it. Vidya stared back at her for a long moment and felt like crying. Even though she was used to Tiffany ignoring her sometimes, she definitely considered Tiffany her best friend forever.

Talk About It

- **Why do you think Tiffany referred to Jenna as her "BFF" right in front of Vidya? Has something like that ever happened to you?**

- **How does it feel to have a friend choose someone else over you?**

- **How do you think Jenna feels in this situation?**

When she and Stacy returned to their post, Stacy said, "Hey, I thought that was mean of Tiffany to say that about Jenna right in front of you. Why do you even hang out with her when she treats you like crap?"

Vidya had never thought about it before. Why did she hang out with Tiffany? She couldn't even choose the movies they saw together, let alone count on her to be her partner in PE class. Come to think of it, she really wasn't that much of a best friend. In that moment, she wanted nothing to do with Tiffany ever again.

"I don't even know. I think I'm just over it," Vidya told Stacy. "I'm just not going to be friends with her anymore."

Talk About It

- Will Vidya stick to her word and not be friends with Tiffany, or will it change when Tiffany gets sick of Jenna and comes around to her again?

- What can Vidya do to stop the on-again, off-again cycle of friendship with Tiffany?

- Have you ever had an on-again, off-again friend? How did the friendship make you feel?

That weekend, Vidya was lonely, so she called Stacy to see if she wanted to go to a movie.

"I'm so glad you called. I was just sitting here at home bored out of my mind," Stacy said. "What do you want to see?"

"I dunno, whatever you want to see is fine," Vidya said halfheartedly. She was so used to letting Tiffany pick that it had become a habit.

"Don't be like that. You pick, and I'll pick next time," Stacy replied.

They ended up seeing the thriller that Vidya had wanted to see for weeks. One scene was so intense that Stacy shrieked out loud in the middle of the theater, sending both girls into giggles. Laughing about it afterward over pizza, Vidya began to think there was more to friendship than just getting into the best parties.

Vidya began to think there was more to friendship than just getting into the best parties.

Sometimes it's hard not to get sucked into an unhealthy friendship, even if it makes you feel sad and unworthy. Vidya bends over backward just to get Tiffany's approval, and sometimes she doesn't even get that. It is far more satisfying to have friendships with people who treat you as an equal than those who cut you down or ignore you. If you find yourself in an unhealthy cycle with an on-and-off friend, it is often better to have no relationship at all.

A good way to tell if a friendship is balanced is to ask yourself how much time you're spending worrying about whether the other person likes you. If it's a lot, then it's probably time to start looking into other options for friends. Once you let go of a friendship with someone who makes you feel bad about yourself, you'll have so much more freedom and time to focus on people who you truly enjoy being around, and who truly enjoy being around you.

Get Healthy

1. If you are a naturally quiet person, accept that about yourself and look for friends who bother to ask what you think rather than talking over your silence. Maybe you will find you have better conversations with girls in smaller groups or one-on-one than you do at parties.

2. Practice disagreeing! If someone asks you if you want pizza for lunch when you'd prefer a hamburger, say so. You may discover that others are prepared to accommodate your wishes just as you would try to accommodate theirs. You shouldn't have to always agree to feel accepted or part of a group.

3. When you start to feel overwhelmed by friends who run the show, remind yourself that you are your own person. Make an effort to convince people to see things your way every once in a while. If not, think about walking away and finding other friends who will consider your ideas.

The Last Word from Ashley

It is a wonderful quality to be an easygoing person and a good listener. But it's not healthy to be so sensitive to others that you ignore your own wishes or instincts. Striking a balance between the two is ideal. Plus, other kids will be more interested in hanging out with you if you bring the fun, instead of just being there. Put it this way: Would you want to hang out with someone who always agrees with everything you say and never has an idea or opinion of her own? If your answer is no, then don't be that way with someone else. Stick up for yourself once in a while! You'll feel better and attract nicer friends.

5

The Dumper

Of course it's important to stand up for what you want and believe in, but is it possible to be too focused on your own desires? Some girls are willing to push other girls around to get what they want. They might manipulate or bully their friends and classmates. If you struggle with being too bossy, you can end up pushing away good friends. Or, if you ditch your friends whenever you're sick of them, eventually they'll wise up and quit hanging out with you.

What is the best way to stay true to yourself while still showing respect to the people who are important to you? In the last chapter, we learned how to avoid being too clingy from Vidya and her problems with her on-again, off-again friend, Tiffany. But we still don't really know what was going on in Tiffany's head, or why she kept blowing off her friends.

Tiffany's Story

Tiffany was a natural leader, and she had no problem saying exactly what she thought in any situation. Her strong personality got her classmates' attention, and her edgy sense of humor kept them laughing. She had a magnetic quality that made people want to be around her.

Because Tiffany never had to try very hard to make friends, she didn't always treat the ones she had as well as they treated her. If she was sick of certain people, she'd usually tell them that they annoyed her straight to their faces. Other times, she'd ignore them for a while until she felt like hanging out again. Take her friend, Vidya, for example. Tiffany knew she sometimes blew Vidya off,

> **Because Tiffany never had to try very hard to make friends, she didn't always treat the ones she had as well as they treated her.**

and she could tell that it hurt her feelings, but she felt like she couldn't help herself. She told herself she was being honest, and that other people should quit trying to be so nice all the time.

Even though she sometimes felt bad about hurting Vidya's feelings, she secretly enjoyed pushing her around. Although she wouldn't admit it to anyone else, she liked getting away with being mean, and she liked having the power in her friendships.

Talk About It

- Is Tiffany being honest when she blows off Vidya or tells people they are annoying?

- How can Tiffany feel bad about hurting Vidya's feelings but enjoy it at the same time?

- Can you think of a time when you enjoyed being mean to another person? What did you like about it?

One day when Tiffany was especially bored with Vidya, she decided to hang out with her friend Jenna instead. Jenna sometimes reminded Tiffany of herself. They both were leaders and trendsetters, and they both could crack a funny joke, even if it was sometimes at the expense of someone else.

One day when Tiffany was especially bored with Vidya, she decided to hang out with her friend Jenna instead.

Before the relay race that day, Tiffany and Jenna were laughing and having a great time. Tiffany noticed Vidya looking unhappy on the other side of the field,

but she didn't let it bother her. In fact, it made her laugh harder. Even when the gym teacher tried to pair the two together, Tiffany went so far as to tell the teacher that she wanted to be with Jenna instead. She even called Jenna her "BFF" right in front of Vidya.

Talk About It

- Why did Tiffany call Jenna her "BFF" in front of Vidya? Was it purely to be mean, or could she have had other reasons?

- Do you have different friends you enjoy hanging out with at different times? How do you avoid hurting anyone's feelings?

- What could Tiffany do instead of ignoring Vidya when she wants to spend time with Jenna?

During gym, Tiffany didn't care at all what Vidya thought, but she thought about it a few days later when she tried to instant message her.

"What R U up 2? I saw Greg's new pic online!" Tiffany wrote, referring to an eighth-grade boy whom Vidya and Tiffany both thought was super hot.

After a few minutes, Vidya still had not responded. Tiffany wrote again, "Hello? Is anyone home??"

She could see that Vidya was online, but there was still no answer.

"Cat got ur tongue?" Tiffany wrote.

"I'm here, but I don't want 2 chat now," was Vidya's reply.

"Y not?" Tiffany wrote back, but a minute later Vidya had logged off.

At first, Tiffany was confused. Why would Vidya not want to talk? Could she have been too busy? Finally, she remembered what happened in gym class and realized that Vidya was probably really mad at her. Tiffany picked up the phone to call her, but when Vidya answered the phone, all she said was, "I can't talk right now. Bye." She didn't sound sad, just frosty.

Tiffany suddenly felt really crummy. She remembered how she'd laughed with Jenna even though Vidya was watching, and she remembered purposely calling Jenna her "BFF" in front of Vidya. She hadn't really meant it. She just wanted to see Vidya's reaction. She figured Vidya would get that it was a joke. And if not, Tiffany assumed Vidya would just get over it.

But that's not what ended up happening. For the first time, Tiffany realized that she might have pushed Vidya to her limit. Maybe Vidya would never want to be friends again, she thought to herself, feeling even worse. Tiffany couldn't think of a time when she had felt like this. She felt bad for herself and for Vidya at the same time. She realized she needed to apologize.

Talk About It

- **Have you ever had a fight with a friend when you felt bad about yourself, but also bad for the other person?**

- **What made Tiffany realize that she needed to apologize?**

That night, Tiffany tried to call Vidya, but she wasn't home. Vidya's mom said she had gone to the movies with Stacy. Tiffany felt weird about that. She was so used to Vidya being available whenever she wanted. She almost felt jealous of Stacy.

The next day, Tiffany stopped by Vidya's house to apologize. Despite what had happened, she really thought Vidya would be happy to see her, but Vidya came to the door with her arms crossed and didn't invite her inside. They stood out on the doorstep.

"Look, I'm sorry, okay?" Tiffany said, feeling awkward and just wanting the whole thing to be over with. "I didn't know that would hurt your feelings so bad. I'm sick of Jenna, and I miss you. Can't we just forget this and hang out again?"

Vidya looked at her coldly. "I can't be your friend just because you're bored and you don't have anyone else to hang out with at the moment," she said. "I have better things to do." Then she turned around and walked back inside.

Talk About It

- Do you think Vidya will ever forgive Tiffany? Should she? Why or why not?

- What could Tiffany do to try to earn back Vidya's friendship?

- Have you ever had a good friendship that ended? What happened, and how did you feel about it?

Ask Dr. Vicki

Even though Tiffany might seem really confident on the outside, and even believes herself to be powerful and in control of other people, she probably has plenty of insecurities inside. Girls who feel the need to push other girls around are often trying to prove something to themselves because they feel inadequate in other ways.

It can feel good to be able to say exactly what you think, regardless of the consequences. The trick is to learn how to be truthful and brave with your words without hurting someone else's feelings, especially someone you truly care about. It's always easier to point out someone else's flaws than to own up to your own. And it can be very difficult to apologize and admit you were wrong. But if you can learn how to recognize when you make mistakes, and share them in an honest way, then you will continue to attract friends who you can keep.

Get Healthy

1. Identify five times when you know you acted mean or unfairly to someone close to you. Now think of five nice things you could do to try to make up for those times. You can start with something small, such as sharing your dessert at lunch, or you can go for something bigger, such as writing an e-mail apologizing to a friend you hurt.

2. If you and your friend are hanging out, take turns deciding what to do. If you choose the movie, let her decide what to eat. She will appreciate having a little control, and you will have an opportunity to try something new.

3. Pay attention to how your actions make you feel inside. If you feel crummy, that's a sign that you need to change your behavior in some way.

4. Say something kind to a girl less popular than you, such as complimenting something she's wearing. Give yourself an opportunity to feel good about treating her as an equal.

The Last Word from Ashley

When people talk about the Mean Girl, they usually forget to mention that she isn't just mean. She is also fun sometimes, and funny other times, and even friendly when she wants to be, just like everyone else. If she weren't, no one would choose to be her friend. Even the nicest of girls can be awful sometimes. Particularly during adolescence, the line between mean and nice gets blurred. So, it's important to check yourself every once in a while. If you lean toward the mean side, recognize that you are not better or worse than anyone else. Enjoy the ways that you are unique and make an effort to appreciate other girls' individuality, too.

6

The Loner

Pretty much all girls have ups and downs with friends during middle school. One day, a girl might have five friends texting her at the same time and a few weeks later end up stuck at home with no one to hang out with on a Friday night. At some point or another, almost every girl finds out how much it hurts to feel like she doesn't have a friend in the world. But most often the lonely feeling passes and she realizes she really does have good friends, or she makes some new ones.

But some girls really don't have any friends. Some girls are naturally less out-going and have more difficulty reaching out to others and making friends. Maybe a girl gets teased so much at school that no one wants to hang out with her. Maybe she has a disability, a weight problem, or acne that crushes her confidence and prevents her from reaching out to new people. Or maybe she chooses to be alone, telling herself she prefers it that way. Most likely, a combination of reasons explains why a girl stays lonely and friendless for months or years at a time. Whatever the reasons, it

Some girls are naturally less outgoing and have more difficulty reaching out to others and making friends.

can be difficult to get through middle school without friends. Being alone can lead to feelings of invisibility and inferiority. Other kids might look down on a loner, making her the target of teasing or bullying.

What's it like to be alone, and how can a girl with no friends break the cycle of loneliness and find some quality people to hang out with? Read on to find out why Talia chooses to keep to herself.

Talia's Story

Talia was a total loner. She hardly spoke to anyone at school, she ate by herself, and she avoided partnering with her classmates for projects. Even at home, she spent most of her time in her room, listening to music or playing on her computer. The only people she would call friends were the ones who played her favorite online games, but even they only interacted in emoticons and instant messages.

Talia's mom tried to get her to come out of her room and spend time with the family. She'd suggest that Talia invite someone over from school. Talia just wasn't very interested in family time or sleepovers, although she could tell it bothered her mom that she spent so much time by herself.

Talk About It

- **Do you like to spend time by yourself, or do you prefer to be with other people?**

- **Do you consider yourself to be a loner?**

- **Why do you think it bothers Talia's mom that she spends so much time by herself?**

Talia hadn't always been such a loner. At her old school she had a bunch of friends. But a year ago she had to transfer when her family moved from one school district to another. At first, she tried hard to get in with the cool groups at her new school. She had wanted friends so badly that she acted a certain way to get attention, such as being really sarcastic in class to try to get people to laugh. At her old school, people thought she was funny, but at the new school, people seemed to hate her. Whenever she said something, it seemed like people rolled their eyes or called her jokes stupid.

It got so bad that she stopped talking at all, for fear that people would just make fun of her. She felt like no one got her sense of humor or understood her. After a while it just seemed to make more sense to hang out alone. She told herself there was no point in bothering with all the jerks.

Now that Talia had been at her new school for some time, she had gotten used to hanging out by herself. She hardly ever thought about what it would be like to call a friend on the phone and invite her over. In fact, she thought most of the other girls' conversations she overheard were just plain stupid. She had once felt like everyone hated her, but now she hated them right back.

The only people in Talia's school she thought might be even slightly cool, or at least not totally dense like everyone else, were a group of kids that everyone called the Scrubs. The Scrubs included a few rocker, skater, and art kids. Talia knew that a few of them also were into online gaming like she was and listened to some of her favorite bands.

Talia was tempted to try talking to them at school, but she didn't want to look like a dork.

Talia was tempted to try talking to them at school, but she didn't want to look like a dork. She didn't want to seem like she was trying too hard. After all, if anyone knew how bad it was to get caught trying too hard, it was Talia.

One day, Talia found herself in a reading group with one of the coolest-looking scrubs. John had long-ish hair and was wearing a T-shirt from a band Talia listened to almost every day. Talia was nervous, but she felt like now might be her only chance to say something to him.

"That's a cool shirt," she said quietly.

"Thanks," John said.

"Have you heard their second album?"

"Yeah, it's good, but I like the first one better," John said.

Talia and John chatted a little bit more about music. The conversation didn't get her invited to any parties that weekend, but it was probably the best time she'd had in months. She felt like a weight had been lifted. Maybe she could find a friend or two after all.

Talk About It

- Why do you think Talia hates her classmates when before she had wanted so badly to make them her friends?

- Can you think of a time when you completely changed your feelings toward someone or a group of people? What made you do that?

- How could Talia break into the Scrubs group without appearing as though she were trying too hard?

Spending so much time alone, Talia was at serious risk for developing depression. After a difficult transition into her new school, she totally lost the social part of her personality and retreated into herself. Part of the problem with being alone for a long time is that kids might get used to it and stop believing that anyone will ever really get them, or stop caring about having friends altogether. When a girl gets to the point of giving up, it can be extra hard for her to find a group or a buddy. That makes it extra important that she work on improving her social life as soon as it starts to go downhill. Caring parents or other role models can be great sources of support as she gets over the hump of unpopularity.

Get Healthy

1. If you find yourself in a situation with a group of kids your own age, look for things that make you want to get to know them better. Odds are that at least one or two of them have something interesting to say. Then, ask them a few simple questions to get a conversation started.

2. You don't have to tell an amazing story or crack a funny joke to get the attention of your classmates. Smiling and saying "hi" usually works just fine.

3. Seek out another girl who seems to be a bit
   shy or quiet. Trying to make friends with her
   might be less scary than trying to sit with
   the most popular girl in school in the lunch-
   room, for example.

The Last Word from Ashley

It can be difficult to have faith in other people
if you've been treated badly and rejected.
Unfortunately, bad experiences tend to affect a
girl's confidence in making and keeping friends.
It is no wonder that she might just not bother
with other people after a while. It's cool to do
your own thing, but don't get so used to it that
you forget how to relate to your peers, or miss
out on doing something fun because you're too
afraid to interact with other people. Remember
that this is your life, so don't let your worries
about what other people think prevent you
from living it to the fullest. There have got to
be some like-minded girls out there who will appreciate you for who you are and not force you
to fake anything. Make it your goal to find out
who they are.

7

The Boy-Crazy Girl

$\mathcal{A}$s you well know, girls can have plenty of trouble relating to each other one-on-one or in groups. But when boys enter the picture, things can get even more complicated. We've all probably known a girl who is a great friend and a blast to be around—until a cute boy shows up. Suddenly, she stops listening to anything you're saying because she's so busy staring at the boy and trying to get his attention. It can be super annoying when a friend zones out like that. Still, most of us have to admit that we've acted a little boy crazy now and then. We can forgive each other for occasional moments of weakness, but when a girl bails on her friends over and over again, it becomes aggravating.

It's important to know how to have fun with a crush or a new boyfriend without making your friends feel unimportant or forgotten. If you're on the other side of the situation, with a friend who is so wrapped up with Mr. Amazing that she can't even remember to call when she says she will,

It's important to know how to have fun with a crush or a new boyfriend without making your friends feel unimportant or forgotten.

you might have to give her a clue about how her behavior is making you feel. Part of the fun of having crushes and starting to date is talking about it with your girlfriends. Of course, that means staying close with your friends even after you've fallen for Prince Charming.

Charlotte learned that lesson the hard way. She was so excited to finally have a boyfriend that she forgot to consider her friends' feelings.

Charlotte's Story

Everyone knew Charlotte was boy crazy. Her friends made fun of her because it seemed like she had a new crush on someone "really cool" every other week. Her typical pattern was to fall for someone out of the blue, talk about him for days straight, then, just as quickly as she'd fallen in love, decide she didn't like him anymore and move on to someone else.

Even though Charlotte's friends teased her, they seemed to have fun gossiping with her about cute boys, especially when they were interested in one of them. Charlotte could get just as excited about her friends' love lives as her own, talking for hours about what Cool Guy wore that day, or whether or not he was making eye contact during class. She even played matchmaker sometimes.

Talk About It

- Are you boy crazy? Or do you know someone who is? What's it like? What do your friends think of it?

- Have you ever had times when you felt obsessed with romance and dating? What was that like?

After all her pining away after various boys, Charlotte finally met someone who seemed to really like her back. His name was Chris, and they met at a youth group camping retreat. Charlotte's friends were happy for her, though they assumed she'd get sick of him as soon as the memories of the campfire began to fade. They were all surprised when two weeks after

they began seeing each other, Charlotte seemed crazier about Chris than ever.

Charlotte's friends started to see less of her because she spent so much time hanging out with Chris or talking to him on the phone. A few times, she didn't show up when she said she was going to. She knew they were a little annoyed, but she didn't feel too bad about it. She thought her friends should just be happy for her that she found someone.

When she did show up, she talked about Chris constantly—the kind of music he liked to listen to, the foods he liked to eat, and the sweet things that he said to her on the phone at night. Charlotte was so wrapped up in Chris that she couldn't even partici-

pate in a regular conversation anymore. If Haylie was talking about the new pair of sandals she just bought, Charlotte would say something like, "Chris has the coolest sneakers!"

Talk About It

- **How do you think Charlotte's friends feel about her new relationship?**

- **Have you ever had a friend get so into a guy that she didn't seem to listen to anything you said? How did that make you feel?**

- **Have you ever been so into a guy that you started to forget about your friends?**

One day, during break, Lynn was telling Charlotte about the new guy she liked.

"He seems really nice, and I think he might like me," Lynn said.

"Well, if he was really that interested, I'm sure he would have called you already," Charlotte said, feeling like an expert on the topic. "Chris always calls me twice a day."

Charlotte knew that what she said might have been a little harsh, but she figured she should tell Lynn the truth so she'd stop following some guy around who obviously wasn't the real thing.

Talk About It

- **Was there anything wrong with what Charlotte said?**

- **Can you remember a time when you gave a friend advice, even though you knew it might not be what she wanted to hear?**

- **Has a friend ever given you advice that you didn't want to hear?**

All of a sudden, Lynn blew up. "You know what, Charlotte? Everyone is getting really sick of you talking about Chris and how great he is all the time. It's like you think you're so cool because you have a boyfriend, but you don't have any friends anymore. When he dumps you, you'll be all alone."

With that Lynn turned and walked away. Charlotte couldn't believe her ears. She felt embarrassed and angry as she screeched at Lynn's back, "You're just jealous because no one will ever like you!"

She felt embarrassed and angry as she screeched at Lynn's back, "You're just jealous because no one will ever like you!"

After her fight with Lynn, Charlotte felt angry and hurt. She told herself that if all her friends were talking about her behind her back, why should she even bother with them? The only thing that made her feel better was her relationship with Chris, and she spent even more time with him.

Despite Chris, Charlotte started to miss her friends. She missed girl talk and sleepovers, and being able to wear sweatpants and complain about her cramps—stuff she just didn't feel as comfortable doing around a guy. Charlotte had to admit that even though her fight with Lynn had hurt, she had been acting kind of distant and cold toward her friends since she got a boyfriend. Now she was worried they wouldn't want anything to do with her. It was time to figure out how to make things right.

Talk About It

- Do you agree with Charlotte's decision not to bother with her friends anymore?

- Once you have a boyfriend, do you still need girlfriends? Why?

- What kinds of things do you feel comfortable doing with your girlfriends that you wouldn't with a boyfriend? Why?

- What might Charlotte do to make things right?

Ask Dr. Vicki

Girls are under a lot of pressure in junior high to be popular, to date, and to be liked by boys. Sometimes girls get so caught up in boys and the idea of having a boyfriend that they lose sight of the most important people in their lives—their friends. Instead of becoming cooler for having a boyfriend, a boy-crazy girl can find herself with fewer friends than before.

Other girls feel jealous and left out as they watch their friends start dating without them. They may start to push their dating friends away because of hurt feelings. Whether or not you are dating, try not to let boys come between you and your girlfriends.

Get Healthy

1. If your friend is being a little distant because she just started dating someone new, cut her a little slack—she'll probably snap out of it in a few weeks. But if she stops calling or hanging out all together, then it might be time for a heart-to-heart.

2. Having a boyfriend is not the answer to all of your problems. If you are insecure about your body, you'll feel that way even if a guy makes out with you. If you feel like you're not good enough by yourself, you probably won't feel good being with someone else.

Don't go out with someone because you need to—do it because you want to.

3. Sometimes friendships have ups and downs. You may not see much of a close friend for a while because one of you is hanging out with other people, boys or girls. Give each other some space, but try to keep a connection.

4. Often, if something is bugging someone, she will make a joke to get her point across. If your friends are constantly teasing you for being boy crazy, ask yourself if there is some truth to what they're saying and think about ways to tone it down a bit.

The Last Word from Ashley

Have you heard that old saying "There are plenty of fish in the sea"? Well, it's true. You'll probably have plenty of love interests during your life, but you may only have a handful of friendships that last. There are so many great experiences to be had with your friends and by yourself that don't involve dating. Even those who do date usually end up seeing many different people before anything really serious comes out of it.

8

The Rebel

As much as some girls would give anything to fit in, other girls would much rather stand out. These girls might do crazy and outrageous things to show that they are not just "one of the crowd." A girl might rebel because she's sick of feeling restricted, or maybe she's just not interested in what's "normal." She might be angry with her family or her peers and want to say or do something that she knows would hurt them or make them uncomfortable. Or, she may have a creative streak that she doesn't know how to express within the limits of a typical adolescent life.

It can be exciting and fun to do something that no one expects you to do, but you have to be careful about what kind of rebellion you select. Getting into risky drug use or sexual behavior as a way to stand out from the crowd is not the best way to make your point and show respect for yourself. As Keisha's story will show you, it's possible to show your individuality and still come out ahead in the end.

It can be exciting and fun to do something that no one expects you to do, but you have to be careful about what kind of rebellion you select.

Keisha's Story

Keisha was one of those girls who acted really tough. She wore dark-colored clothes—some of which she bought in the boys' department—lots of black eye makeup, and heavy jewelry. At school and at home she usually said exactly what she thought at any moment, even if it could get her into trouble. She didn't care if people thought she was rude. Actually, she kind of enjoyed being thought of as a rebel.

Even though Keisha was naturally smart, she tended to do poorly in school and was usually put in the remedial classes. She skated by without doing her homework but managed to get decent scores on tests.

Keisha came from a single-parent home, with a mom who worked late and partied later, so she didn't have many rules. When she wasn't in school, she hung out with a group of tough guys in her neighborhood. She was the only girl, and they usually talked to her like

she was one of the guys, cursing and giving her a hard time. Keisha considered them to be her only friends. She knew they'd have her back if anyone messed with her, and she felt safe with them.

Talk About It

- Can you think of reasons why Keisha might enjoy being thought of as rude?

- Have you ever enjoyed being a rebel? What did you enjoy about it? How did other people react to your behavior?

- Have you ever judged someone based on a first impression? Were you right?

One night they were all hanging out at Darnell's apartment when his parents weren't home. Mike and Darnell pulled out a joint and lit up. They passed it over to Keisha, and she decided to try it. She was a little nervous because she'd never smoked weed before, but she pretended it was no big deal. Darnell must have known she was nervous, though, because he was acting extra sweet, showing her how to hold it and everything.

Talk About It

- Do you know anyone who drinks or does drugs? How do you feel about it?

- Has anyone ever offered you weed or another drug? If so, what did you do? If not, what would you do in this situation?

Pretty soon Keisha started to feel light-headed and tingly, and she realized she must be getting high. She felt scared, but she also couldn't stop giggling. Darnell and Mike were laughing, too, and watching her. Darnell grabbed her hand and was holding it. Keisha liked holding his hand.

Then, all of a sudden, Darnell was kissing Keisha and putting his hands under her shirt. Keisha knew Mike was sitting right there. She didn't want to be kissing Darnell in front of him, or kissing him at all. But she felt so weird and high that she didn't know how to stop it. She felt scared because she didn't like what Darnell was doing and because she felt so out of it. Normally, she'd have just shoved him off and called him an idiot. After a few minutes, she wiggled away from him, and they all sat watching television until Keisha felt normal enough to walk home.

Talk About It

- Why was Keisha scared? Why didn't she just push Darnell away?

- Has a guy ever tried to get too physical with you in a way that made you uncomfortable or scared? What did you do about it?

- Have you ever tried to do anything to get high? Why did you do it, and how did it make you feel?

Once Keisha got home and went to her room, she realized her heart was pounding and she felt super anxious and not giggly at all anymore. It took her a long time to fall asleep, and when she woke up in the morning, she was overcome with a sense of dread. Why had Darnell kissed her like that, right in front of Mike? She felt angry with him for kissing her and touching

her when she couldn't even think straight. It seemed as if he didn't care that she wasn't into it, and that made her feel dirty and used. She also was angry with herself for smoking weed in the first place.

After that night, Keisha didn't smoke weed with the boys again. She didn't feel safe around them like she used to. She felt uncomfortable about her body, and she hid it by wearing even more boyish clothes than before.

Talk About It

- **How would you feel toward Darnell if you were Keisha? How would you feel toward Mike?**

- **Can you think of a time when you were angry with yourself for doing something? What did you do? What about it made you angry?**

- **Why was Keisha uncomfortable about her body? Have you ever felt like that?**

One day at school, a counselor came to talk to the girls about sexual violence. The woman ran support groups for girls who had been sexually abused. She told them that many women and girls are molested or raped during their lifetimes, maybe as many as one out of three. When she was talking, Keisha kept thinking about the night with Darnell and Mike, and she started to get upset. It just seemed so unfair that girls should have to worry about guys putting their hands on their bodies.

Even though Keisha usually ignored adults or mouthed off to them, she decided to talk to the counselor after class. She wanted to tell her how good she thought the talk was and how unfair it was that girls had to worry about that stuff all the time. The counselor was cool and seemed genuinely interested in hearing what Keisha thought. She even invited Keisha to an upcoming march to protest violence against

women. It wasn't the kind of thing that Keisha usually got into, but she really liked this woman, and she felt strongly about the issue. Keisha decided to go.

Talk About It

- Have you ever made an effort to talk to a teacher or another adult because you respected what they had to say? How did they respond?

- Would you ever attend a protest, march, or rally to raise awareness about an issue that you cared about? What do you think it would be like?

- Have you ever been molested or sexually abused? What happened? Did you tell someone? Why or why not?

When Keisha showed up at the march, hundreds of girls and women of all different ages were there. Some of them looked pretty normal, while others were wearing weird or tough-looking outfits. The thing they all had in common, though, was that they all seemed really pumped to be there. They marched through part of the city with signs and chanted stuff about women's rights to keep their bodies safe.

At first Keisha was a little uncomfortable with the chanting, but after a while she got into it and started throwing her fists in the air with everyone else.

At first Keisha was a little uncomfortable with the chanting, but after a while she got into it and started throwing her fists in the air with everyone else. It was like an emotional release after what happened to her. Keisha felt better than she had in months.

Talk About It

- **What do you think marching and chanting accomplishes?**

- **Why do you think attending the protest made Keisha feel better?**

- **How has Keisha changed since before her bad experience with Darnell? Is she still a rebel?**

Ask Dr. Vicki

Keisha tried to make people pay attention to her by dressing tough, being loud and rude in class, and hanging out with kids who were doing dangerous and illegal things. She got so carried away with rebelling that she failed to keep herself safe from harm. The problem with having friends who reject authority figures is that you can end up distancing yourself from anyone who might be able to help you if you found yourself in a dangerous position.

It is okay to rebel sometimes, but make sure that you're doing it for the right reasons. Kids who choose to act out usually are struggling with deeper issues that they have trouble facing. For example, it's possible that Keisha was acting tough because inside she was feeling lonely, rejected, and angry with her parents for not being there for her. In reality, acting out doesn't really make up for the hurt that fuels the rebel's behavior, and it can lead to dangerous situations.

Get Healthy

1. If you feel like you don't belong, or you don't even want to belong, try to identify what exactly you don't like about the mainstream. Respond to the specific things you don't like, instead of rejecting entire groups of people. If you don't like girls who act too girly, look

for ones with qualities you admire, such as athleticism or toughness. Use those opportunities to get to know people you otherwise might have written off.

2. Don't tell yourself you don't care what other people think of you. Everyone cares what people think of them on some level. Sometimes, the girls who say this are the ones who cared the most, and got hurt. So, they try to deny how they feel to protect themselves from getting hurt again.

3. If someone does something to you or your body that scares you or makes you uncomfortable, immediately talk to an adult you can trust. Realize that sexual or other violations are never acceptable and never your fault.

The Last Word from Ashley

Unfortunately, sexual violence is a threat to all girls, especially throughout adolescence and young adulthood. No matter how tough a girl is, she still can find herself at risk for being sexually violated. If she does drugs, drinks, or hangs out with other people who do, that risk increases. Be careful to establish limits for yourself. If something is illegal or makes you feel uncomfortable, scared, or dirty, that is an excellent sign that it is beyond a healthy level of rebellion.

9

The Hot Date

Long gone are the days when you and your friends thought of boys as gross. These days, you're probably thinking just the opposite—somehow the boys who not so long ago were laughing at their burps and roughhousing on the playground have become more attractive and interesting. You might be looking at them as potential friends or boyfriends, and you're probably becoming curious about dating, kissing, and being touched.

At the same time, you might also be feeling nervous and uneasy about your changing feelings toward boys. Maybe it seems like all your friends have started dating, and you even hear about girls your age who are "hooking up." If you're not one of them, you might feel left out or less cool. If you have started dating, that can be even more unnerving. You'll have to start making decisions about what you're comfortable doing and probably will spend a lot of time second-guessing yourself. How far should you go? What's normal? Will he still like you if you don't let him touch your breasts or take your clothes off?

You'll have to start making decisions about what you're comfortable doing. How far should you go? What's normal?

Amber thought she was ready to date, even if her parents disagreed. But after going behind her parents' backs to date an older boy, she discovered she may have gotten herself in over her head.

Amber's Story

Amber had gone from ecstatic to furious in under an hour. Tyler, a guy she met hanging out at the pool, had just asked her out. He was so hot—a football player, with beautiful blue eyes and a great tan. He made her laugh every time she saw him. Plus, he was a freshman in high school. Amber was only in the eighth grade, and she couldn't believe she'd been asked out by a high school guy!

But of course, her super lame parents had said no when she asked them if she could date him.

"Yeah, right," her mom said.

"You're way too young. No way," her dad added.

"You're kidding me! I'm 14," Amber protested. "That's not too young. My friends are all dating. Why can't I?"

"What your friends do is none of our concern because they're not our daughter," her mom said. "You know better. We've always said, you can't date until you're 16."

"It's not fair! I hate you!" Amber yelled and stormed off to her room.

Talk About It

- **Do you think Amber is too young to date? What's a good age to start dating?**

- **Do your parents let you date? What are the rules?**

- **How else could Amber have handled this conversation?**

In her room, Amber laid on her bed, furious. She knew her parents were wrong. They were just old-fashioned. Girls were far more mature these days, and they just didn't get that. Well, she wasn't going to let that stop her. Why did they even have to know? Besides, she had already told Tyler that she'd meet him at the movies Friday evening.

When Friday came around, Amber told her mom that she was seeing a movie with her friend Bridget. Bridget's older sister was going to pick her up. At least that last part was true—it was just that Bridget and her sister were going to drop her off at the theater to meet up with Tyler.

"Just make sure you're back by curfew," her mom said.

"Okaaay, Mom," said Amber, sounding annoyed.

"Hey. I know you're still mad at me for not letting you go out with that boy, but I want you to understand something," her mom said as Amber put on her coat. "We don't make these rules just to spite you. We're looking out for you because we care."

But Amber was already running out the door. "I gotta go, Mom! They're here."

Talk About It

- What did Amber's mother mean when she said they make the rules because they care?

- What do you think of Amber's plan? Could anything go wrong?

- Have you ever lied to your parents about where you were going or who you'd be hanging out with? What happened?

Amber's plan worked perfectly that night, and she went out with Tyler two other times using a similar strategy. She liked Tyler more and more, and he seemed to be really into her, too. By the third date, she barely saw any of the movie because they spent most of the time making out.

That night after the movie, Tyler asked her if she wanted to walk over to his friend Matt's house. "His parents don't get home until late, so it's a good place to hang out," Tyler said, smiling at her so sweetly. "Come on, I want to get to know you. He has a car, and I'm sure he'll drive you home later if that's what you're worried about."

Amber looked at her watch. She still had an hour and a half until she had to be home, and she wanted to keep getting to know Tyler, too. So she called Bridget and told her she wouldn't need a ride after all.

Talk About It

- Why do you think Tyler wants to take Amber to his friend's house?

- Should Amber go with him? Why might this be a bad decision?

- Have you ever spent time alone with a boy you were dating? What happened?

Matt let them in, then went back to playing a video game in the other room. Tyler took Amber's hand and led her downstairs, where they were alone. Without turning on the light, Tyler started kissing her passionately. Then he started putting his hands all over her and pulling at her clothes.

Amber felt a chill of excitement and fear. She wasn't sure how far Tyler wanted to go, and more importantly, she wasn't sure how far she wanted to go. She really wanted him to like her and was afraid he would think she was immature if she didn't go along with him. Frantically, she tried to think of what to do.

Ask Dr. Vicki

Just like Amber, you may find that when you are with a guy, you feel a "chill of excitement and fear." It's the battle between your hormones saying "go for it" and your voice of reason saying "slow down." While it feels good to be held, kissed, and touched, just remember that you have the right to say "that's enough" every step of the way. Any boy who does not respect your decisions is not worth having as a boyfriend.

This is just as true for gay relationships. Just because you can't get pregnant doesn't mean that the risks of sexually transmitted diseases aren't still there, and you still have to make decisions about what you are comfortable and uncomfortable doing. Respect is important in any relationship.

Get Healthy

1. Instead of dating one-on-one, go out in groups. You'll probably feel more comfortable with your other friends around and still have a chance to get to know the boy you like. And if you're not alone with him, you'll be less likely to be pressured into doing something you don't want to do.

2. If your parents won't let you date, consider that you might have different ideas of what dating means. Maybe you just mean hanging

out with a guy in a group, while your parents are picturing you making out in the back-seat of someone's car. Talk it over calmly with them and come to an understanding of what is and isn't allowed.

3. Don't be in a hurry to do too much too fast. You have years ahead of you to experience everything you might think you're missing out on now. And the more mature you are, the more you will probably enjoy that inter-action when it eventually happens.

The Last Word from Ashley

Dating can be lots of fun, but becoming sexu-ally active is serious business. One poor deci-sion could change the course of your life—with a child to care for, an abortion or an adoption to agonize over, a disease that affects your health and your sex life, or the trauma of forced physi-cal interaction. Even if none of that happens, you'll have to deal with the emotional fallout. Girls often feel used and regretful if they go further than they're ready to. Many girls avoid these issues by choosing abstinence.

Not all guys will try to take advantage of you, but that doesn't mean you shouldn't be careful. Decide ahead of time what you are and are not comfortable doing. That way if you're put in a tough spot, you won't be making a hasty decision in the heat of the moment.

A Second Look

If there's one thing the stories in this book can teach us, it's that managing your social life is no easy task. Your best friend could become your enemy. You could be pressured to do something you know is wrong, because it's dangerous, illegal, or could hurt someone's feelings. Or you could find yourself without any social life whatsoever.

Whatever challenges you face—you're likely to face more than a few—can become opportunities for you to learn something about yourself, your friends, or even the people you thought were your friends. If you learn how much it sucks to get dumped by a group, maybe you'll choose not to dump someone else. Or if you make a choice that puts you in a dangerous situation, you'll know to make a better choice next time.

The lessons you learn during adolescence will come in handy later on. Thinking about what's most important to you in a friendship will help prepare you to meet new people and make better choices in friends and dating partners. Plus, you will start to think about the friend you want to be and learn to treat people like you want to be treated.

Most importantly, you will see how spending time with honest and caring people and basing your friendships on trust are really ways of being good to yourself. After all, sometimes you've got to be your own best friend.

XOXO,
Ashley

Pay It Forward

Remember, a healthful life is about balance. Now that you know how to walk that path, pay it forward to a friend or even to yourself! Remember the Get Healthy tips throughout this book, and then take these steps to get healthy and get going.

- Practice standing up for yourself and for your friends. If someone is pressuring you to do something that doesn't feel right, have the courage to stick up for yourself.

- Friends can come from unexpected places, so try getting to know different kinds of people. You'll probably meet someone interesting, and you won't have to rely on the approval of one particular group to feel good about yourself.

- Think about the most important qualities a friend should have. Then ask yourself, if a friend had all these qualities, would that person's gender, race, religion, or sexual orientation matter?

- Treat others the way you would like to be treated. Before you talk about another girl behind her back, put yourself in her place. If someone else is spreading the rumor, consider sticking up for the girl. People will respect you more if you are kind to everyone.

- If you always find yourself going along with what other people say or want, practice disagreeing! You're more likely to get their respect, not to mention get your own way sometimes.

- Think of a few times when you treated someone unkindly. Now think of a few nice things you could do to offset them.

- Talk to a girl who is less popular than you. Say something nice and ask her about herself. You never know—you might make a new, interesting friend!

- If making friends is difficult for you, try smiling and saying "hi" more often. You'll find that little things go a long way toward getting people to see you in a more positive light.

- Recognize that friendships have their ups and downs. If a close friend drifts away for a while because of a new boyfriend, a busy schedule, or family drama, cut her some slack. In the meantime, try to keep in touch in little ways, such as with a weekly phone call or an e-mail.

- If you think you have been violated, sexually or otherwise, tell an adult you trust. While girls should be careful to look out for their own safety, sexual violations are never acceptable and never your fault.

Additional Resources

Selected Bibliography

Rubin, Kenneth H. *The Friendship Factor: Helping Our Children Navigate Their Social World—And Why It Matters to Their Success*. New York: Viking Penguin, 2002.

Simmons, Rachel. *Odd Girl Out: The Hidden Culture of Aggression in Girls*. Orlando: Harvest Books, 2003.

Thompson, Michael, et al. *Best Friends, Worst Enemies: Understanding the Social Lives of Children*. New York: Ballantine Books, 2001.

Yager, Jan. *When Friendship Hurts: How to Deal with Friends Who Betray, Abandon, or Wound You*. New York: Fireside, 2002.

Further Reading

Desetta, Al, ed. *The Courage to be Yourself: True Stories by Teens About Cliques, Conflicts, and Peer Pressure*. Minneapolis: Free Spirit Publishing, 2005.

Kirberger, Kimberly, and Colin Mortensen. *On Friendship: A Book for Teenagers*. Deerfield Beach, FL: Health Communications, 2000.

Musgrave, Susan, ed. *You Be Me: Friendship in the Lives of Teen Girls*. Toronto: Annick Press, 2002.

Web Sites

To learn more about friendship and dating, visit ABDO Publishing Company on the World Wide Web at **www.abdopublishing.com**. Web sites about friendship and dating are featured on our Book Links page. These links are routinely monitored and updated to provide the most current information available.

For More Information

Girls, Inc.
120 Wall Street New York, NY 10005-3902
800-374-4475
www.girlsinc-online.org/members/Welcome.html
A leader in the girls' rights movement, this leadership group offers online support and information as well as advocacy movements in the nation's capital.

This Is Me, Inc.
4315 North Richmond, #1S, Chicago, IL 60618
773-539-4901
www.thisismeinc.org
This nonprofit organization provides guidance to adolescent girls as they explore their identities and discover their individual strengths.

Glossary

abstinence
A choice not to engage in sexual activity.

approval
The act or instance of thinking that someone or something is acceptable or good.

assault
To violently attack someone or something.

compromise
An agreement that is reached after people with opposing views each give up something of their demands.

confident
Having a strong belief in your own abilities.

cycle
A series of events that is repeated over and over again.

devastating
Shocking and distressing.

gay
Romantically interested in people of the same gender.

gossip
Idle talk about other people's business.

intimidate
To frighten or threaten someone.

magnetic
Possessing an unusual power or ability to attract.

molest
To force someone to engage in physical and usually sexual contact.

popular
Having many friends or being liked by many people.

pressure
Strong influence, force, or persuasion.

rape
To force someone to have sexual intercourse.

rebel
Someone who fights against the people in charge of something.

remedial
Intended to help or correct something.

trust
The belief that someone is honest and reliable.

victim
A person who is hurt, killed, or made to suffer.

violation
The act or instance of treating someone or something with great disrespect.

Index

About the Author

Ashley Rae Harris lives and works in Chicago, Illinois. She received a master of arts degree from the University of Chicago. Her research focused on how internet culture has impacted adolescent girls' body image and sense of identity. Her work has appeared in *VenusZine* and *Time Out Chicago*. She enjoys live music, bike riding, and spending time with the many friends whose experiences helped her write this book.

Photo Credits

Lauren Greenfield/AP Images, 12; Jupiterimages/AP Images, 16; Carmen Martínez; Banús/iStock Photo, 19; Rich Legg/iStock Photo, 25; Eileen Hart/iStock Photo, 27; Tracy Whiteside/iStock Photo, 29; Matt Henry Gunther/Getty Images, 35; Joselito Briones/iStock Photo, 37; iStock Photo, 46; Izabela Habur/iStock Photo, 48; Brad Wieland/iStock Photo, 55; iStock Photo, 59; Joseph C. Justice Jr./iStock Photo, 65; Baerbel Schmidt/Getty Images, 66; James Darell/Getty Images, 73; Chris Schmidt/iStock Photo, 74; Hola Images/Getty Images, 77; Lauren Greenfield/AP Images, 82; Jim Pruitt/iStock Photo, 85; Joyce Naltchayan/Getty Images, 87; Quavondo Nguyen/iStock Photo, 89; Renee Lee/iStock Photo, 95; iStock Photo, 97; George Doyle/Getty Images, 99